TRUTH OVER LIES

LOVEGODGREATLY.COM

A Word to Parents

This book grew out of a desire to provide
a companion study journal for children
to use alongside the *Truth Over Lies* adult
study journal and book.

Love God Greatly is dedicated to making
God's Word available to our beautiful
community of women... and now, women
have the opportunity to share God's Word
with children through this study uniquely
crafted for young hearts.

CONTENTS

INTRODUCTION
TRUTH OVER LIES

Have you heard your parents, teachers, or grandparents talk about how easy you have it today? It used to be much harder for people to find answers, to buy something, or to plan a vacation without the internet, smart phones, and social media.

If the older people in your life wanted to know something - like how much rain falls in tropical rainforests, how many teeth sharks have, or how slow sloths move - it was much harder for them. To find the truth, they had to clear time after work, put gas in the car, drive to the library, ask the librarian, search through a card catalog to find the book title they needed, then locate it on the shelf and read it until they found an answer. When they found the answer, they felt triumphant and excited to know something, like how happy you are after winning a game!

Now you can type a question into Google and get an answer in less than a second! Do you get the same sense of excitement when you learn something new? There is a big difference today. It is much easier to find information, but the flood of information actually makes life harder.

Years ago, the books people used to find answers in were heavily researched before they were written, extensively checked while they were written, and tirelessly edited after they were written. It took a long time to print books and put them on display on bookshelves because no one wanted to write anything that was untrue. Now, people can write anything they want and it is accessible to everyone in the world. Meanwhile, God wants us to read *His* Word and discover the Truth.

You are God's precious creation! He knew everything about you before He knitted you in your mother's womb and He knows everything about you now. And He loves you! *God created you because He thought the world needed one of you!* And there is only one of you. How amazing is that?

God also knows when you hurt. He feels your pain when words or actions from people around you, or things you see or hear on television, make you feel like you will never be good enough or make you think you will never be noticed. Those are lies. God says you are fearfully and wonderfully made and He knows your heart and notices your every move!

You are growing every day. God planted you like a seed on earth and every day you are sprouting and getting taller. Our Almighty God wants you to grow into a mighty tree. If you want that too, you will need strong roots planted in His Truth! When you are mighty, your big, beautiful green leaves will shade those beneath you from the scorching sun. When you are mighty, you will be healthy and produce delicious fruit that will feed and enrich others. When you are mighty, you will not fold or break in a storm. If you want to be mighty, you must learn how to plant yourself in God's Truth.

"THEY WILL BE LIKE A TREE PLANTED BY THE WATER THAT SENDS OUT ITS ROOTS BY THE STREAM. IT DOES NOT FEAR WHEN HEAT COMES; ITS LEAVES ARE ALWAYS GREEN. IT HAS NOT WORRIES IN A YEAR OF DROUGHT AND NEVER FAILS TO BEAR FRUIT." JEREMIAH 17:8

As you grow taller each day, God will use this study to teach you how to grow strong too. He will remove lies trying to hold you down and free you to live the wonderful life He has planned for you! Let us open His Book and grow together so we can live victorious lives!

READING PLAN

WEEK 1

WHO IS SPEAKING
THESE LIES & WHY?

Monday - Satan Tries to Deceive Us
Read: Genesis 3:1-4; John 8:44; Ephesians 6:11
SOAP: John 8:44; Ephesians 6:11

Tuesday - Satan Hates God & His People
Read: Acts 13:10; Revelation 12:10; 2 Thessalonians 3:3
SOAP: Revelation 12:10; 2 Thessalonians 3:3

Wednesday - We Can Deceive Ourselves
Read: Jeremiah 17:9-10; 1 Corinthians 3:18; Ezekiel 36:26
SOAP: Jeremiah 17:9-10

Thursday - We Can Be Deceived by Loving the World
Read: 1 John 5:19; 1 John 2:15-16; Colossians 2:8; 2 Timothy 3:13-14
SOAP: Colossians 2:8

Friday - We Can Be Deceived Through Our Ignorance
Read: 1 John 4:1; 1 Thessalonians 5:21; Acts 17:11; Psalm 119:11; Titus 3:3-6; James 1:22
SOAP: Psalm 119:11

WEEK 2

LIES ABOUT GOD

Monday - You Have to Earn God's Love
Read: Ephesians 2:8; 1 John 4:19
SOAP: Ephesians 2:8

Tuesday - God is Not Enough
Read: Philippians 4:19; Psalm 73:23-26; 2 Corinthians 12:9
SOAP: Philippians 4:19; 2 Corinthians 12:9

Wednesday - God Puts Shame and Guilt on You as Punishment
Read: Isaiah 54:4-5; Romans 8:1
SOAP: Romans 8:1

Thursday - God is Stingy
Read: Romans 8:31-32; John 1:16; James 1:5; Ephesians 1:3-8
SOAP: Romans 8:31-32

Friday - God Won't Forgive You for That...
Read: Isaiah 43:25; 1 John 1:9
SOAP: Isaiah 43:25; 1 John 1:9

WEEK 3

LIES ABOUT YOU (PART 1)

Monday - You Are Not Enough
Read: Exodus 3:1-14; Exodus 4:1-11; 1 Peter 2:9; Philippians 4:13; Ephesians 2:10
SOAP: Exodus 4:11

Tuesday - You Can't Change
Read: Hebrews 13:20-21; Philippians 4:13
SOAP: Hebrews 13:20-21

Wednesday - You Aren't Loved
Read: Romans 8:37-39; Romans 5:8
SOAP: Romans 5:8

Thursday - You Need to Rely on Your Own Strength
Read: 1 Corinthians 1:26-31; Proverbs 3:5-6; Isaiah 40:28-31; Jeremiah 17:5-8
SOAP: Proverbs 3:5-6

Friday - You're Too Old/Young to be Used by God
Read: Job 12:12; Psalm 92:12-14; 1 Timothy 4:12
SOAP: Psalm 92:12-14; 1 Timothy 4:12

WEEK 4

LIES ABOUT YOU (PART 2)

Monday - My Life is About Me
Read: Isaiah 43:1-7; Matthew 5:16; 1 Corinthians 10:31
SOAP: Isaiah 43:7

Tuesday - My Failure Defines Me
Read: 2 Corinthians 12:9-10; 1 Peter 2:9-10
SOAP: 1 Peter 2:9-10

Wednesday - My Success Defines Me
Read: Proverbs 16:18; John 15:5; James 1:17
SOAP: John 15:5

Thursday - I Can't be Confident in
the Things God has Called Me to Do
Read: 2 Corinthians 3:4-5
SOAP: 2 Corinthians 3:4-5

Friday - I Am a Victim
Read: Genesis 50:19-21; 1 Peter 2:22-23; Philippians 1:12-14;
Psalms 10:14; Isaiah 43:18-19
SOAP: Isaiah 43:18-19

WEEK 5
LIES ABOUT HAPPINESS

Monday - Money Brings Happiness
Read: Ecclesiastes 5:10; Hebrews 13:5
SOAP: Hebrews 13:5

Tuesday - Possessions Bring Happiness
Read: Matthew 6:19-21; Luke 12:15; Ecclesiastes 3:11
SOAP: Matthew 6:19-21

Wednesday - Beauty & Health Bring Happiness
Read: 2 Corinthians 4:16-18; Proverbs 31:30; Psalm 39:4
SOAP: 2 Corinthians 4:16-18

Thursday - Happiness Can Not Be Found in Trials
Read: James 1:2-4,12; Romans 5:3-5; 1 Peter 4:12-13
SOAP: James 1:2-4

Friday - Happiness Can Be Found Apart from God
Read: Psalm 144:15; Psalm 68:3; Psalm 146:5; Psalm 4:6-7; Hebrews 1:9
SOAP: Psalm 4:6-7

WEEK 6
OVERCOMING THE LIES

Monday - Arm Yourself
Read: Ephesians 6:11-17
SOAP: Ephesians 6:11

Tuesday - Learn Wisdom
Read: Proverbs 13:20; James 1:5
SOAP: James 1:5

Wednesday - Walk in Truth
Read: John 8:31-32; John 17:17
SOAP: John 8:31-32

Thursday - Pray for Discernment
Read: Psalm 25:5; Psalm 119:6
SOAP: Psalm 25:5

Friday - Think on What is True
Read: Romans 12:2; Philippians 4:8
SOAP: Philippians 4:8

YOUR GOALS

We believe it's important to write out goals for this study. Take some time now and write three goals you would like to focus on as you begin to rise each day and dig into God's Word. Make sure and refer back to these goals throughout the next weeks to help you stay focused. You can do it!

1.

2.

3.

Signature:

Date:

PRAYER

WRITE DOWN YOUR PRAYER REQUESTS AND PRAISES FOR EACH DAY.

Prayer focus for this week:
Spend time praying for your family members.

MONDAY

TUESDAY

WEDNESDAY

THURSDAY

FRIDAY

WEEK 1
Who Is Speaking These Lies & Why?

See to it that no one takes you captive by philosophy and empty deceit, according to human tradition, according to the elemental spirits of the world, and not according to Christ.

Colossians 2:8

SCRIPTURE FOR WEEK 1

MONDAY

Genesis 3:1-4

1 Now the serpent was more crafty than any other beast of the field that the LordGod had made.

He said to the woman, "Did God actually say, 'You shall not eat of any tree in the garden'?" 2 And the woman said to the serpent, "We may eat of the fruit of the trees in the garden, 3 but God said, 'You shall not eat of the fruit of the tree that is in the midst of the garden, neither shall you touch it, lest you die.'" 4 But the serpent said to the woman, "You will not surely die.

John 8:44

44 You are of your father the devil, and your will is to do your father's desires. He was a murderer from the beginning, and does not stand in the truth, because there is no truth in him. When he lies, he speaks out of his own character, for he is a liar and the father of lies.

Ephesians 6:11

11 Put on the whole armor of God, that you may be able to stand against the schemes of the devil.

TUESDAY

Acts 13:10

10 and said, "You son of the devil, you enemy of all righteousness, full of all deceit and villainy, will you not stop making crooked the straight paths of the Lord?

Revelation 12:10

10 And I heard a loud voice in heaven, saying, "Now the salvation and the power and the kingdom of our God and the authority of his Christ have come, for the accuser of our brothers has been thrown down, who accuses them day and night before our God.

2 Thessalonians 3:3

3 But the Lord is faithful. He will establish you and guard you against the evil one.

WEDNESDAY

Jeremiah 17:9-10

9 The heart is deceitful above all things,
and desperately sick;
who can understand it?
10 "I the Lord search the heart
and test the mind,
to give every man according to his ways,
according to the fruit of his deeds."

1 Corinthians 3:18

18 Let no one deceive himself. If anyone among you thinks that he is wise in this age, let him become a fool that he may become wise.

Ezekiel 36:26

26 And I will give you a new heart, and a new spirit I will put within you. And I will remove the heart of stone from your flesh and give you a heart of flesh.

THURSDAY

1 John 5:19

19 We know that we are from God, and the whole world lies in the power of the evil one.

1 John 2:15-16

15 Do not love the world or the things in the world. If anyone loves the world, the love of the Father is not in him. 16 For all that is in the world—the desires of the flesh and the desires of the eyes and pride of life—is not from the Father but is from the world.

Colossians 2:8

8 See to it that no one takes you captive by philosophy and empty deceit, according to human tradition, according to the elemental spirits of the world, and not according to Christ.

2 Timothy 3:13-14

13 while evil people and impostors will go on from bad to worse, deceiving and being deceived. 14 But as for you, continue in what you have learned and have firmly believed, knowing from whom you learned it.

FRIDAY

1 John 4:1

1 Beloved, do not believe every spirit, but test the spirits to see whether they are from God, for many false prophets have gone out into the world.

1 Thessalonians 5:21

21 but test everything; hold fast what is good.

Acts 17:11

11 Now these Jews were more noble than those in Thessalonica; they received the word with all eagerness, examining the Scriptures daily to see if these things were so.

Psalm 119:11

11 I have stored up your word in my heart,
   that I might not sin against you.

Titus 3:3-6

3 For we ourselves were once foolish, disobedient, led astray, slaves to various passions and pleasures, passing our days in malice and envy, hated by others and hating one another. 4 But when the goodness and loving kindness of God our Savior appeared, 5 he saved us, not because of works done by us in righteousness, but according to his own mercy, by the washing of regeneration and renewal of the Holy Spirit, 6 whom he poured out on us richly through Jesus Christ our Savior.

James 1:22

22 But be doers of the word, and not hearers only, deceiving yourselves.

MONDAY

Read:
Genesis 3:1-4; John 8:44; Ephesians 6:11

SOAP:
John 8:44; Ephesians 6:11

1. Write out today's **SCRIPTURE** passage.

_____

_____

_____

_____

_____

_____

_____

_____

_____

_____

2. On the blank page to the right, **DRAW** or **WRITE** what this passage means to you.

3. My **PRAYER** for today:

_____

_____

_____

_____

_____

TUESDAY

Read:
Acts 13:10; Revelation 12:10; 2 Thessalonians 3:3
SOAP:
Revelation 12:10; 2 Thessalonians 3:3

1. Write out today's **SCRIPTURE** passage.

_____

_____

_____

_____

_____

_____

_____

_____

_____

_____

2. On the blank page to the right, **DRAW** or **WRITE** what this passage means to you.

3. My **PRAYER** for today:

_____

_____

_____

_____

_____

_____

WEDNESDAY

Jeremiah 17:9-10; 1 Corinthians 3:18; Ezekiel 36:26
SOAP:
Jeremiah 17:9-10

1. Write out today's **SCRIPTURE** passage.

_____

_____

_____

_____

_____

_____

_____

_____

_____

2. On the blank page to the right, **DRAW** or **WRITE** what this passage means to you.

3. My **PRAYER** for today:

_____

_____

_____

_____

_____

THURSDAY

Read:
1 John 5:19; 1 John 2:15-16; Colossians 2:8; 2 Timothy 3:13-14

SOAP:
Colossians 2:8

1. Write out today's **SCRIPTURE** passage.

_____

_____

_____

_____

_____

_____

_____

_____

_____

_____

_____

2. On the blank page to the right, **DRAW** or **WRITE** what this passage means to you.

3. My **PRAYER** for today:

_____

_____

_____

_____

_____

FRIDAY

Read:
1 John 4:1; 1 Thessalonians 5:21; Acts 17:11; Psalm 119:11; Titus 3:3-6; James 1:22

SOAP:
Psalm 119:11

1. Write out today's **SCRIPTURE** passage.

_____

_____

_____

_____

_____

_____

_____

_____

_____

_____

2. On the blank page to the right, **DRAW** or **WRITE** what this passage means to you.

3. My **PRAYER** for today:

_____

_____

_____

_____

_____

THIS WEEK I LEARNED...

USE THE SPACE BELOW TO DRAW A PICTURE OR WRITE ABOUT WHAT YOU LEARNED THIS WEEK FROM YOUR TIME IN GOD'S WORD.

PRAYER

WRITE DOWN YOUR PRAYER REQUESTS
AND PRAISES FOR EACH DAY.

Prayer focus for this week:
Spend time praying for your country.

MONDAY

TUESDAY

WEDNESDAY

THURSDAY

FRIDAY

WEEK 2
Lies About God

For of His fullness we have
all received, grace upon grace.

John 1:16

SCRIPTURE FOR WEEK 2

MONDAY

Ephesians 2:8

8 For by grace you have been saved through faith. And this is not your own doing; it is the gift of God,

1 John 4:19

19 We love because he first loved us.

TUESDAY

Philippians 4:19

19 And my God will supply every need of yours according to his riches in glory in Christ Jesus.

Psalm 73:23-26

23 Nevertheless, I am continually with you;
   you hold my right hand.
24 You guide me with your counsel,
   and afterward you will receive me to glory.
25 Whom have I in heaven but you?
   And there is nothing on earth that I desire besides you.
26 My flesh and my heart may fail,
   but God is the strength of my heart and my portion forever.

2 Corinthians 12:9

9 But he said to me, "My grace is sufficient for you, for my power is made perfect in weakness." Therefore I will boast all the more gladly of my weaknesses, so that the power of Christ may rest upon me.

WEDNESDAY

Isaiah 54:4-5

4 "Fear not, for you will not be ashamed;
   be not confounded, for you will not be disgraced;
for you will forget the shame of your youth,
   and the reproach of your widowhood you will remember no more.
5 For your Maker is your husband,
   the Lord of hosts is his name;
and the Holy One of Israel is your Redeemer,
   the God of the whole earth he is called.

Romans 8:1

1 There is therefore now no condemnation for those who are in Christ Jesus.

THURSDAY

Romans 8:31-32

31 What then shall we say to these things? If God is for us, who can be against us? 32 He who did not spare his own Son but gave him up for us all, how will he not also with him graciously give us all things?

John 1:16

16 For from his fullness we have all received, grace upon grace.

James 1:5

5 If any of you lacks wisdom, let him ask God, who gives generously to all without reproach, and it will be given him.

Ephesians 1:3-8

3 Blessed be the God and Father of our Lord Jesus Christ, who has blessed us in Christ with every spiritual blessing in the heavenly places, 4 even as he chose us in him before the foundation of the world, that we should be holy and blameless before him. In love 5 he predestined us for adoption to himself as sons through Jesus Christ, according to the purpose of his will,6 to the praise of his glorious grace, with which he has blessed us in the Beloved. 7 In him we have redemption through his blood, the forgiveness of our trespasses, according to the riches of his grace, 8 which he lavished upon us, in all wisdom and insight.

FRIDAY

Isaiah 43:25

25 "I, I am he
   who blots out your transgressions for my own sake,
   and I will not remember your sins.

1 John 1:9

9 If we confess our sins, he is faithful and just to forgive us our sins and to cleanse us from all unrighteousness.

MONDAY

Read:
Ephesians 2:8; 1 John 4:19

SOAP:
Ephesians 2:8

1. Write out today's **SCRIPTURE** passage.

_____

_____

_____

_____

_____

_____

_____

_____

2. On the blank page to the right, **DRAW** or **WRITE** what this passage means to you.

3. My **PRAYER** for today:

_____

_____

_____

_____

_____

_____

TUESDAY

Read:
Philippians 4:19; Psalm 73:23-26; 2 Corinthians 12:9

SOAP:
Philippians 4:19; 2 Corinthians 12:9

1. Write out today's **SCRIPTURE** passage.

_____

_____

_____

_____

_____

_____

_____

_____

_____

_____

2. On the blank page to the right, **DRAW** or **WRITE** what this passage means to you.

3. My **PRAYER** for today:

_____

_____

_____

_____

_____

WEDNESDAY

Read:
Isaiah 54:4-5; Romans 8:1
SOAP:
Romans 8:1

1. Write out today's **SCRIPTURE** passage.

_____

_____

_____

_____

_____

_____

_____

_____

_____

_____

_____

2. On the blank page to the right, **DRAW** or **WRITE** what this passage means to you.

3. My **PRAYER** for today:

_____

_____

_____

_____

_____

_____

THURSDAY

Read:
Romans 8:31-32; John 1:16; James 1:5; Ephesians 1:3-8
SOAP:
Romans 8:31-32

1. Write out today's **SCRIPTURE** passage.

_____

_____

_____

_____

_____

_____

_____

_____

_____

2. On the blank page to the right, **DRAW** or **WRITE** what this passage means to you.

3. My **PRAYER** for today:

_____

_____

_____

_____

_____

FRIDAY

Read:
Isaiah 43:25; 1 John 1:9

SOAP:
Isaiah 43:25; 1 John 1:9

1. Write out today's **SCRIPTURE** passage.

_____

_____

_____

_____

_____

_____

_____

_____

_____

2. On the blank page to the right, **DRAW** or **WRITE** what this passage means to you.

3. My **PRAYER** for today:

_____

_____

_____

_____

_____

THIS WEEK I LEARNED...

USE THE SPACE BELOW TO DRAW A PICTURE OR WRITE ABOUT WHAT YOU LEARNED THIS WEEK FROM YOUR TIME IN GOD'S WORD.

PRAYER

WRITE DOWN YOUR PRAYER REQUESTS AND PRAISES FOR EACH DAY.

Prayer focus for this week:
Spend time praying for your friends.

MONDAY

TUESDAY

WEDNESDAY

THURSDAY

FRIDAY

WEEK 3
Lies About You (Part 1)

Let no one despise you for your youth,
but set the believers an example
in speech, in conduct, in love,
in faith, in purity.

1 Timothy 4:12

SCRIPTURE FOR WEEK 3

MONDAY

Exodus 3:1-14

1 Now Moses was keeping the flock of his father-in-law, Jethro, the priest of Midian, and he led his flock to the west side of the wilderness and came to Horeb, the mountain of God. 2 And the angel of the Lord appeared to him in a flame of fire out of the midst of a bush. He looked, and behold, the bush was burning, yet it was not consumed. 3 And Moses said, "I will turn aside to see this great sight, why the bush is not burned." 4 When the Lordsaw that he turned aside to see, God called to him out of the bush, "Moses, Moses!" And he said, "Here I am." 5 Then he said, "Do not come near; take your sandals off your feet, for the place on which you are standing is holy ground." 6 And he said, "I am the God of your father, the God of Abraham, the God of Isaac, and the God of Jacob." And Moses hid his face, for he was afraid to look at God.

7 Then the Lord said, "I have surely seen the affliction of my people who are in Egypt and have heard their cry because of their taskmasters. I know their sufferings, 8 and I have come down to deliver them out of the hand of the Egyptians and to bring them up out of that land to a good and broad land, a land flowing with milk and honey, to the place of the Canaanites, the Hittites, the Amorites, the Perizzites, the Hivites, and the Jebusites. 9 And now, behold, the cry of the people of Israel has come to me, and I have also seen the oppression with which the Egyptians oppress them.10 Come, I will send you to Pharaoh that you may bring my people, the children of Israel, out of Egypt." 11 But Moses said to God, "Who am I that I should go to Pharaoh and bring the children of Israel out of Egypt?" 12 He said, "But I will be with you, and this shall be the sign for you, that I have sent you: when you have brought the people out of Egypt, you shall serve God on this mountain."

13 Then Moses said to God, "If I come to the people of Israel and say to them, 'The God of your fathers has sent me to you,' and they ask me, 'What is his name?' what shall I say to them?"14 God said to Moses, "I am who I am." And he said, "Say this to the people of Israel: 'I am has sent me to you.'"

Exodus 4:1-11

1 Then Moses answered, "But behold, they will not believe me or listen to my voice, for they will say, 'The Lord did not appear to you.'" 2 The Lord said to him, "What is that in your hand?" He said, "A staff." 3 And he said, "Throw it on the ground." So he threw it on the ground, and it became a serpent, and Moses ran from it. 4 But the Lord said to Moses, "Put out your hand and catch it by the tail"—so he put out his hand and caught it, and it became

a staff in his hand— 5 "that they may believe that the Lord, the God of their fathers, the God of Abraham, the God of Isaac, and the God of Jacob, has appeared to you." 6 Again, the Lord said to him, "Put your hand inside your cloak." And he put his hand inside his cloak, and when he took it out, behold, his hand was leprous like snow. 7 Then God said, "Put your hand back inside your cloak." So he put his hand back inside his cloak, and when he took it out, behold, it was restored like the rest of his flesh. 8 "If they will not believe you," God said, "or listen to the first sign, they may believe the latter sign. 9 If they will not believe even these two signs or listen to your voice, you shall take some water from the Nile and pour it on the dry ground, and the water that you shall take from the Nile will become blood on the dry ground."

10 But Moses said to the Lord, "Oh, my Lord, I am not eloquent, either in the past or since you have spoken to your servant, but I am slow of speech and of tongue." 11 Then the Lord said to him, "Who has made man's mouth? Who makes him mute, or deaf, or seeing, or blind? Is it not I, the Lord?

1 Peter 2:9

9 But you are a chosen race, a royal priesthood, a holy nation, a people for his own possession, that you may proclaim the excellencies of him who called you out of darkness into his marvelous light.

Philippians 4:13

13 I can do all things through him who strengthens me.

Ephesians 2:10

10 For we are his workmanship, created in Christ Jesus for good works, which God prepared beforehand, that we should walk in them.

TUESDAY

Hebrews 13:20-21

20 Now may the God of peace who brought again from the dead our Lord Jesus, the great shepherd of the sheep, by the blood of the eternal covenant, 21 equip you with everything good that you may do his will, working in us that which is pleasing in his sight, through Jesus Christ, to whom be glory forever and ever. Amen.

Philippians 4:13

13 I can do all things through him who strengthens me.

WEDNESDAY

Romans 8:37-39

37 No, in all these things we are more than conquerors through him who loved us. 38 For I am sure that neither death nor life, nor angels nor rulers, nor things present nor things to come, nor powers, 39 nor height nor depth, nor anything else in all creation, will be able to separate us from the love of God in Christ Jesus our Lord.

Romans 5:8

8 but God shows his love for us in that while we were still sinners, Christ died for us.

THURSDAY

1 Corinthians 1:26-31

26 For consider your calling, brothers: not many of you were wise according to worldly standards, not many were powerful, not many were of noble birth. 27 But God chose what is foolish in the world to shame the wise; God chose what is weak in the world to shame the strong; 28 God chose what is low and despised in the world, even things that are not, to bring to nothing things that are, 29 so that no human being might boast in the presence of God. 30 And because of him you are in Christ Jesus, who became to us wisdom from God, righteousness and sanctification and redemption, 31 so that, as it is written, "Let the one who boasts, boast in the Lord."

Proverbs 3:5-6

5 Trust in the Lord with all your heart,
   and do not lean on your own understanding.
6 In all your ways acknowledge him,
   and he will make straight your paths.

Isaiah 40:28-31

28 Have you not known? Have you not heard?
The Lord is the everlasting God,
   the Creator of the ends of the earth.
He does not faint or grow weary;
   his understanding is unsearchable.
29 He gives power to the faint,
   and to him who has no might he increases strength.
30 Even youths shall faint and be weary,
   and young men shall fall exhausted;

31 but they who wait for the Lord shall renew their strength;
    they shall mount up with wings like eagles;
they shall run and not be weary;
    they shall walk and not faint.

Jeremiah 17:5-8

5 Thus says the Lord:
"Cursed is the man who trusts in man
    and makes flesh his strength,
        whose heart turns away from the Lord.
6 He is like a shrub in the desert,
    and shall not see any good come.
He shall dwell in the parched places of the wilderness,
    in an uninhabited salt land.
7 "Blessed is the man who trusts in the Lord,
    whose trust is the Lord.
8 He is like a tree planted by water,
    that sends out its roots by the stream,
and does not fear when heat comes,
    for its leaves remain green,
and is not anxious in the year of drought,
    for it does not cease to bear fruit."

FRIDAY

Job 12:12

12 Wisdom is with the aged,
    and understanding in length of days.

Psalm 92:12-14

12 The righteous flourish like the palm tree
    and grow like a cedar in Lebanon.
13 They are planted in the house of the Lord;
    they flourish in the courts of our God.
14 They still bear fruit in old age;
    they are ever full of sap and green,

1 Timothy 4:12

12 Let no one despise you for your youth, but set the believers an example in speech, in conduct, in love, in faith, in purity.

MONDAY

Read:
Exodus 3:1-14; Exodus 4:1-11; 1 Peter 2:9; Philippians 4:13; Ephesians 2:10
SOAP:
Exodus 4:11

1. Write out today's **SCRIPTURE** passage.

_____

_____

_____

_____

_____

_____

_____

_____

_____

2. On the blank page to the right, **DRAW** or **WRITE** what this passage means to you.

3. My **PRAYER** for today:

_____

_____

_____

_____

_____

TUESDAY

Hebrews 13:20-21; Philippians 4:13
SOAP:
Hebrews 13:20-21

1. Write out today's **SCRIPTURE** passage.

_____

_____

_____

_____

_____

_____

_____

_____

_____

_____

2. On the blank page to the right, **DRAW** or **WRITE** what this passage means to you.

3. My **PRAYER** for today:

_____

_____

_____

_____

_____

WEDNESDAY

Read:
Romans 8:37-39; Romans 5:8
SOAP:
Romans 5:8

1. Write out today's **SCRIPTURE** passage.

_____

_____

_____

_____

_____

_____

_____

_____

_____

2. On the blank page to the right, **DRAW** or **WRITE** what this passage means to you.

3. My **PRAYER** for today:

_____

_____

_____

_____

_____

THURSDAY

1 Corinthians 1:26-31; Proverbs 3:5-6; Isaiah 40:28-31; Jeremiah 17:5-8

SOAP:
Proverbs 3:5-6

1. Write out today's **SCRIPTURE** passage.

_____

_____

_____

_____

_____

_____

_____

_____

_____

_____

2. On the blank page to the right, **DRAW** or **WRITE** what this passage means to you.

3. My **PRAYER** for today:

_____

_____

_____

_____

_____

_____

FRIDAY

Read:
Job 12:12; Psalm 92:12-14; 1 Timothy 4:12

SOAP:
Psalm 92:12-14; 1 Timothy 4:12

1. Write out today's **SCRIPTURE** passage.

_____

_____

_____

_____

_____

_____

_____

_____

_____

2. On the blank page to the right, **DRAW** or **WRITE** what this passage means to you.

3. My **PRAYER** for today:

_____

_____

_____

_____

_____

THIS WEEK I LEARNED...

USE THE SPACE BELOW TO DRAW A PICTURE OR WRITE ABOUT WHAT YOU LEARNED THIS WEEK FROM YOUR TIME IN GOD'S WORD.

PRAYER

WRITE DOWN YOUR PRAYER REQUESTS AND PRAISES FOR EACH DAY.

Prayer focus for this week:
Spend time praying for your church.

MONDAY

TUESDAY

WEDNESDAY

THURSDAY

FRIDAY

WEEK 4
Lies About You (Part 2)

But he said to me, "My grace is sufficient for you, for my power is made perfect in weakness." Therefore I will boast all the more gladly of my weaknesses, so that the power of Christ may rest upon me. For the sake of Christ, then, I am content with weaknesses, insults, hardships, persecutions, and calamities. For when I am weak, then I am strong.

2 Corinthians 12:9-10

SCRIPTURE FOR WEEK 4

MONDAY

Isaiah 43:1-7

1 But now thus says the Lord,
he who created you, O Jacob,
   he who formed you, O Israel:
"Fear not, for I have redeemed you;
   I have called you by name, you are mine.
2 When you pass through the waters, I will be with you;
   and through the rivers, they shall not overwhelm you;
when you walk through fire you shall not be burned,
   and the flame shall not consume you.
3 For I am the Lord your God,
   the Holy One of Israel, your Savior.
I give Egypt as your ransom,
   Cush and Seba in exchange for you.
4 Because you are precious in my eyes,
   and honored, and I love you,
I give men in return for you,
   peoples in exchange for your life.
5 Fear not, for I am with you;
   I will bring your offspring from the east,
   and from the west I will gather you.
6 I will say to the north, Give up,
   and to the south, Do not withhold;
bring my sons from afar
   and my daughters from the end of the earth,
7 everyone who is called by my name,
   whom I created for my glory,
   whom I formed and made."

Matthew 5:16

16 In the same way, let your light shine before others, so that they may see your good works and give glory to your Father who is in heaven.

1 Corinthians 10:31

31 So, whether you eat or drink, or whatever you do, do all to the glory of God.

TUESDAY

2 Corinthians 12:9-10

9 But he said to me, "My grace is sufficient for you, for my power is made perfect in weakness." Therefore I will boast all the more gladly of my weaknesses, so that the power of Christ may rest upon me. 10 For the sake of Christ, then, I am content with weaknesses, insults, hardships, persecutions, and calamities. For when I am weak, then I am strong.

1 Peter 2:9-10

9 But you are a chosen race, a royal priesthood, a holy nation, a people for his own possession, that you may proclaim the excellencies of him who called you out of darkness into his marvelous light. 10 Once you were not a people, but now you are God's people; once you had not received mercy, but now you have received mercy.

WEDNESDAY

Proverbs 16:18

18 Pride goes before destruction,
    and a haughty spirit before a fall.

John 15:5

5 I am the vine; you are the branches. Whoever abides in me and I in him, he it is that bears much fruit, for apart from me you can do nothing.

James 1:17

17 Every good gift and every perfect gift is from above, coming down from the Father of lights, with whom there is no variation or shadow due to change.

THURSDAY

2 Corinthians 3:4-5

4 Such is the confidence that we have through Christ toward God. 5 Not that we are sufficient in ourselves to claim anything as coming from us, but our sufficiency is from God,

FRIDAY

Genesis 50:19-21

19 But Joseph said to them, "Do not fear, for am I in the place of God? 20 As for you, you meant evil against me, but God meant it for good, to bring it about that many people[a] should be kept alive, as they are today. 21 So do not fear; I will provide for you and your little ones." Thus he comforted them and spoke kindly to them.

1 Peter 2:22-23

22 He committed no sin, neither was deceit found in his mouth.23 When he was reviled, he did not revile in return; when he suffered, he did not threaten, but continued entrusting himself to him who judges justly.

Philippians 1:12-14

12 I want you to know, brothers, that what has happened to me has really served to advance the gospel, 13 so that it has become known throughout the whole imperial guard and to all the rest that my imprisonment is for Christ. 14 And most of the brothers, having become confident in the Lord by my imprisonment, are much more bold to speak the word without fear.

Psalms 10:14

14 But you do see, for you note mischief and vexation,
    that you may take it into your hands;
to you the helpless commits himself;
    you have been the helper of the fatherless.

Isaiah 43:18-19

18 "Remember not the former things,
    nor consider the things of old.
19 Behold, I am doing a new thing;
    now it springs forth, do you not perceive it?
I will make a way in the wilderness
    and rivers in the desert.

MONDAY

Read:
Isaiah 43:1-7; Matthew 5:16; 1 Corinthians 10:31
SOAP:
Isaiah 43:7

1. Write out today's **SCRIPTURE** passage.

_____

_____

_____

_____

_____

_____

_____

_____

_____

_____

2. On the blank page to the right, **DRAW** or **WRITE** what this passage means to you.

3. My **PRAYER** for today:

_____

_____

_____

_____

_____

_____

TUESDAY

Read:
2 Corinthians 12:9-10; 1 Peter 2:9-10
SOAP:
1 Peter 2:9-10

1. Write out today's **SCRIPTURE** passage.

_____

_____

_____

_____

_____

_____

_____

_____

_____

2. On the blank page to the right, **DRAW** or **WRITE** what this passage means to you.

3. My **PRAYER** for today:

_____

_____

_____

_____

_____

WEDNESDAY

Read:
Proverbs 16:18; John 15:5; James 1:17
SOAP:
John 15:5

1. Write out today's **SCRIPTURE** passage.

_____

_____

_____

_____

_____

_____

_____

_____

_____

_____

_____

2. On the blank page to the right, **DRAW** or **WRITE** what this passage means to you.

3. My **PRAYER** for today:

_____

_____

_____

_____

_____

_____

THURSDAY

Read:
2 Corinthians 3:4-5
SOAP:
2 Corinthians 3:4-5

1. Write out today's **SCRIPTURE** passage.

_____

_____

_____

_____

_____

_____

_____

_____

_____

2. On the blank page to the right, **DRAW** or **WRITE** what this passage means to you.

3. My **PRAYER** for today:

_____

_____

_____

_____

_____

FRIDAY

Read:
Genesis 50:19-21; 1 Peter 2:22-23; Philippians 1:12-14; Psalms 10:14; Isaiah 43:18-19
SOAP:
Isaiah 43:18-19

1. Write out today's **SCRIPTURE** passage.

_____

_____

_____

_____

_____

_____

_____

_____

2. On the blank page to the right, **DRAW** or **WRITE** what this passage means to you.

3. My **PRAYER** for today:

_____

_____

_____

_____

_____

THIS WEEK I LEARNED...

USE THE SPACE BELOW TO DRAW A PICTURE OR WRITE ABOUT WHAT YOU LEARNED THIS WEEK FROM YOUR TIME IN GOD'S WORD.

PRAYER

WRITE DOWN YOUR PRAYER REQUESTS AND PRAISES FOR EACH DAY.

Prayer focus for this week:
Spend time praying for your church.

MONDAY

TUESDAY

WEDNESDAY

THURSDAY

FRIDAY

WEEK 5
Lies About Happiness

And he said to them, "Take care, and be on your guard against all covetousness, for one's life does not consist in the abundance of his possessions."

Luke 12:15

SCRIPTURE FOR WEEK 5

MONDAY

Ecclesiastes 5:10

10 He who loves money will not be satisfied with money, nor he who loves wealth with his income; this also is vanity.

Hebrews 13:5

5 Keep your life free from love of money, and be content with what you have, for he has said, "I will never leave you nor forsake you."

TUESDAY

Matthew 6:19-21

19 "Do not lay up for yourselves treasures on earth, where moth and rust destroy and where thieves break in and steal, 20 but lay up for yourselves treasures in heaven, where neither moth nor rust destroys and where thieves do not break in and steal. 21 For where your treasure is, there your heart will be also.

Luke 12:15

15 And he said to them, "Take care, and be on your guard against all covetousness, for one's life does not consist in the abundance of his possessions."

Ecclesiastes 3:11

11 He has made everything beautiful in its time. Also, he has put eternity into man's heart, yet so that he cannot find out what God has done from the beginning to the end.

WEDNESDAY

2 Corinthians 4:16-18

16 So we do not lose heart. Though our outer self is wasting away, our inner self is being renewed day by day. 17 For this light momentary affliction is preparing for us an eternal weight of glory beyond all comparison, 18 as we look not to the things that are seen but to the things that are unseen. For the things that are seen are transient, but the things that are unseen are eternal.

Proverbs 31:30

30 Charm is deceitful, and beauty is vain,
   but a woman who fears the Lord is to be praised.

Psalm 39:4

4 "O Lord, make me know my end
   and what is the measure of my days;
   let me know how fleeting I am!

THURSDAY

James 1:2-4,12

2 Count it all joy, my brothers, when you meet trials of various kinds, 3 for you know
that the testing of your faith produces steadfastness. 4 And let steadfastness have its full
effect, that you may be perfect and complete, lacking in nothing. 12 Blessed is the man who
remains steadfast under trial, for when he has stood the test he will receive the crown of
life, which God has promised to those who love him.

Romans 5:3-5

3 Not only that, but we rejoice in our sufferings, knowing that suffering produces
endurance, 4 and endurance produces character, and character produces hope, 5 and hope
does not put us to shame, because God's love has been poured into our hearts through the
Holy Spirit who has been given to us.

1 Peter 4:12-13

12 Beloved, do not be surprised at the fiery trial when it comes upon you to test you, as
though something strange were happening to you. 13 But rejoice insofar as you share Christ's
sufferings, that you may also rejoice and be glad when his glory is revealed.

FRIDAY

Psalm 144:15

15 Blessed are the people to whom such blessings fall!
   Blessed are the people whose God is the Lord!

Psalm 68:3

3 But the righteous shall be glad;
   they shall exult before God;
   they shall be jubilant with joy!

Psalm 146:5

5 Blessed is he whose help is the God of Jacob,
   whose hope is in the Lord his God,

Psalm 4:6-7

6 There are many who say, "Who will show us some good?
   Lift up the light of your face upon us, O Lord!"
7 You have put more joy in my heart
   than they have when their grain and wine abound.

Hebrews 1:9

9 You have loved righteousness and hated wickedness;
therefore God, your God, has anointed you
   with the oil of gladness beyond your companions.

MONDAY

Read:
Ecclesiastes 5:10; Hebrews 13:5

SOAP:
Hebrews 13:5

1. Write out today's **SCRIPTURE** passage.

_____

_____

_____

_____

_____

_____

_____

_____

_____

2. On the blank page to the right, **DRAW** or **WRITE** what this passage means to you.

3. My **PRAYER** for today:

_____

_____

_____

_____

_____

TUESDAY

1. Write out today's **SCRIPTURE** passage.

_____

_____

_____

_____

_____

_____

_____

_____

_____

_____

2. On the blank page to the right, **DRAW** or **WRITE** what this passage means to you.

3. My **PRAYER** for today:

_____

_____

_____

_____

_____

_____

WEDNESDAY

Read:
2 Corinthians 4:16-18; Proverbs 31:30; Psalm 39:4
SOAP:
2 Corinthians 4:16-18

1. Write out today's **SCRIPTURE** passage.

_____

_____

_____

_____

_____

_____

_____

_____

_____

2. On the blank page to the right, **DRAW** or **WRITE** what this passage means to you.

3. My **PRAYER** for today:

_____

_____

_____

_____

_____

THURSDAY

Read:
James 1:2-4,12; Romans 5:3-5; 1 Peter 4:12-13
SOAP:
James 1:2-4

1. Write out today's **SCRIPTURE** passage.

_____

_____

_____

_____

_____

_____

_____

_____

_____

_____

2. On the blank page to the right, **DRAW** or **WRITE** what this passage means to you.

3. My **PRAYER** for today:

_____

_____

_____

_____

_____

_____

FRIDAY

Read:
Psalm 144:15; Psalm 68:3; Psalm 146:5; Psalm 4:6-7; Hebrews 1:9

SOAP:
Psalm 4:6-7

1. Write out today's **SCRIPTURE** passage.

_____

_____

_____

_____

_____

_____

_____

_____

_____

_____

2. On the blank page to the right, **DRAW** or **WRITE** what this passage means to you.

3. My **PRAYER** for today:

_____

_____

_____

_____

_____

THIS WEEK I LEARNED...

USE THE SPACE BELOW TO DRAW A PICTURE OR WRITE ABOUT WHAT YOU LEARNED THIS WEEK FROM YOUR TIME IN GOD'S WORD.

PRAYER

WRITE DOWN YOUR PRAYER REQUESTS AND PRAISES FOR EACH DAY.

Prayer focus for this week:
Spend time praying for your church.

MONDAY

TUESDAY

WEDNESDAY

THURSDAY

FRIDAY

WEEK 6
Overcoming the Lies

Guide me in your truth and teach me,

for you are God my Savior,

and my hope is in you all day long.

Psalm 25:5

SCRIPTURE FOR WEEK 6

MONDAY

Ephesians 6:11-17

11 Put on the whole armor of God, that you may be able to stand against the schemes of the devil. 12 For we do not wrestle against flesh and blood, but against the rulers, against the authorities, against the cosmic powers over this present darkness, against the spiritual forces of evil in the heavenly places. 13 Therefore take up the whole armor of God, that you may be able to withstand in the evil day, and having done all, to stand firm. 14 Stand therefore, having fastened on the belt of truth, and having put on the breastplate of righteousness, 15 and, as shoes for your feet, having put on the readiness given by the gospel of peace. 16 In all circumstances take up the shield of faith, with which you can extinguish all the flaming darts of the evil one; 17 and take the helmet of salvation, and the sword of the Spirit, which is the word of God,

TUESDAY

Proverbs 13:20

20 Whoever walks with the wise becomes wise,
   but the companion of fools will suffer harm.

James 1:5

5 If any of you lacks wisdom, let him ask God, who gives generously to all without reproach, and it will be given him.

WEDNESDAY

John 8:31-32

31 So Jesus said to the Jews who had believed him, "If you abide in my word, you are truly my disciples, 32 and you will know the truth, and the truth will set you free."

John 17:17

17 Sanctify them in the truth; your word is truth.

THURSDAY

Psalm 25:5

5 Lead me in your truth and teach me,
    for you are the God of my salvation;
    for you I wait all the day long.

Psalm 119:6

6 Then I shall not be put to shame,
    having my eyes fixed on all your commandments.

FRIDAY

Romans 12:2

2 Do not be conformed to this world, but be transformed by the renewal of your mind, that by testing you may discern what is the will of God, what is good and acceptable and perfect.

Philippians 4:8

8 Finally, brothers, whatever is true, whatever is honorable, whatever is just, whatever is pure, whatever is lovely, whatever is commendable, if there is any excellence, if there is anything worthy of praise, think about these things.

MONDAY

Ephesians 6:11-17

SOAP:
Ephesians 6:11

1. Write out today's **SCRIPTURE** passage.

_____

_____

_____

_____

_____

_____

_____

_____

_____

2. On the blank page to the right, **DRAW** or **WRITE** what this passage means to you.

3. My **PRAYER** for today:

_____

_____

_____

_____

_____

TUESDAY

Proverbs 13:20; James 1:5

SOAP:
James 1:5

1. Write out today's **SCRIPTURE** passage.

_____

_____

_____

_____

_____

_____

_____

_____

_____

_____

2. On the blank page to the right, **DRAW** or **WRITE** what this passage means to you.

3. My **PRAYER** for today:

_____

_____

_____

_____

_____

WEDNESDAY

Read:
John 8:31-32; John 17:17
SOAP:
John 8:31-32

1. Write out today's **SCRIPTURE** passage.

_____

_____

_____

_____

_____

_____

_____

_____

_____

2. On the blank page to the right, **DRAW** or **WRITE** what this passage means to you.

3. My **PRAYER** for today:

_____

_____

_____

_____

_____

_____

THURSDAY

Read:
Psalm 25:5; Psalm 119:6

SOAP:
Psalm 25:5

1. Write out today's **SCRIPTURE** passage.

_____

_____

_____

_____

_____

_____

_____

_____

_____

2. On the blank page to the right, **DRAW** or **WRITE** what this passage means to you.

3. My **PRAYER** for today:

_____

_____

_____

_____

_____

FRIDAY

Read:
Romans 12:2; Philippians 4:8

SOAP:
Philippians 4:8

1. Write out today's **SCRIPTURE** passage.

_____

_____

_____

_____

_____

_____

_____

_____

_____

_____

2. On the blank page to the right, **DRAW** or **WRITE** what this passage means to you.

3. My **PRAYER** for today:

_____

_____

_____

_____

_____

THIS WEEK I LEARNED...

USE THE SPACE BELOW TO DRAW A PICTURE OR WRITE ABOUT WHAT YOU LEARNED THIS WEEK FROM YOUR TIME IN GOD'S WORD.

Made in the USA
Monee, IL
25 January 2020